I Can Read About™

Seasons

Written by Robyn Supraner • Illustrated by David Henderson

Consultant: Eileen C. Stegemann, Technical Writer,
New York State Department of Environmental Conservation

Spring, summer, autumn, winter—this is the story of the seasons. It is the story of the Earth's never-ending journey around the blazing sun.

Spring

Summer

Day and night, month after month, the Earth travels around the sun. This special journey brings us the seasons of the year. It takes the Earth about 365 days—a year—to complete a single trip. When that trip is done, a new one begins. And the cycle of the seasons begins all over again!

Winter

Autumn

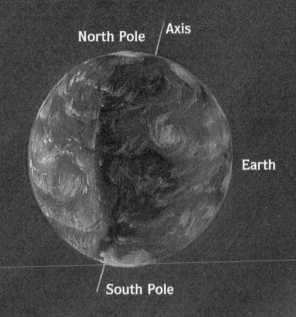

North Pole

Axis

South Pole

Earth

What causes the seasons? It is the Earth's position as it travels around the sun that brings the changing seasons.

To understand this, imagine a straight line running through the Earth from the North Pole to the South Pole. Scientists call this imaginary line the Earth's *axis*.

Summer

Autumn

   Look at how the Earth and
its axis tilt. As the Earth circles
the sun, the tilt of the Earth's
axis does not change; the Earth
always leans in the same direction.
So at certain points along the Earth's journey, the North Pole tilts
away from the sun. When this happens, the northern part of the
Earth, which is called the Northern Hemisphere, gets less sunlight.
At this time, we have winter.

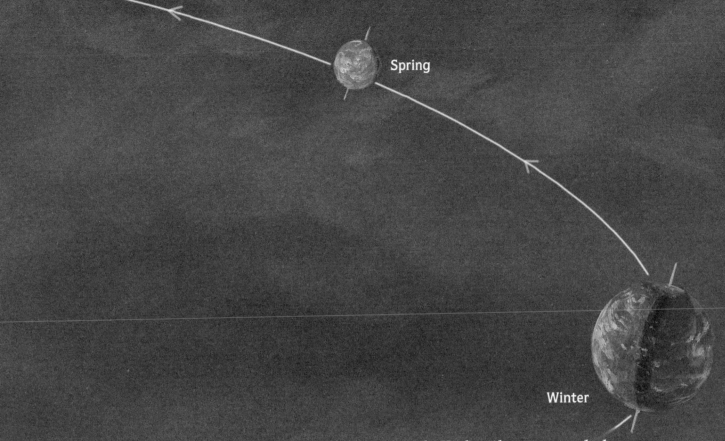

Spring

Winter

At other times along the journey, the North Pole tilts toward the sun. Then, in the north, we get more sunlight, and we have summer. Spring and autumn occur in between these times. In spring, the Northern Hemisphere begins to tilt toward the sun. In autumn, the Northern Hemisphere begins to tilt away from the sun.

Let's follow the Earth on its trip around the sun. We'll explore each of the seasons as it occurs in the Northern Hemisphere.

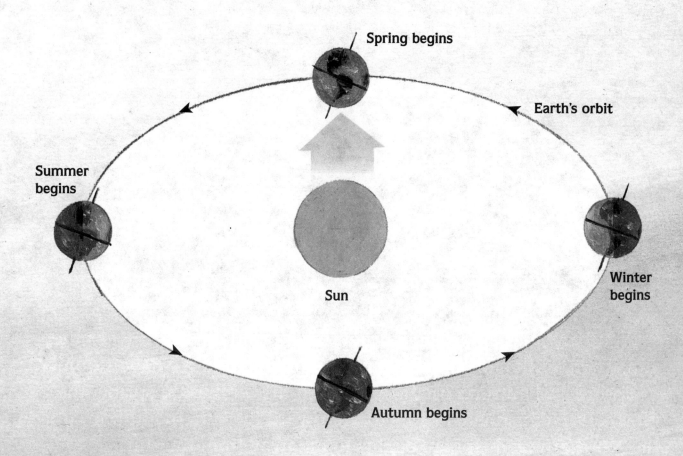

Spring is a good place to start, for spring is a time of beginnings. Spring arrives on March 20 or 21. On that day, the sun's rays shine directly over the *equator*. The equator is the imaginary line that circles the widest part of the Earth between the North and South Poles. On the first day of spring, we have an equal number of hours of daylight and darkness. After that, the days begin to grow longer. Warm sunshine melts the last snow and thaws the frozen ground.

Crocuses pop up. Sap rises in the trees. Once again, thirsty roots carry food and water to branches and buds. Spring is a time of new life.

As April showers gently fall, worms tunnel through the soil. Buds grow fat and burst into flower. Leaves cover the trees.

The warmer weather of spring means it is time for the birds that traveled south for the winter to return to their summer homes in the north. This seasonal journey is called *migration*.

From as far away as South America, some swallows travel more than 7,000 miles (11,270 kilometers) to North America. Orioles return from Mexico. Snow geese can be seen flying north to their summer breeding grounds. Scarlet tanagers come north from Peru. And from the southern part of the United States, many robins fly north.

The birds have returned to their summer homes to build their nests, lay their eggs, and raise their babies.

The worms and insects and berries that will be needed to feed the baby birds are already growing.

During spring, farmers turn the soil and plant seeds in the soft earth. Spring is a time for sowing.

It is also a time of birth. Tiny rabbits blink their eyes and breathe the sweet spring air. They are getting their first look at the world.

Young lambs play in the green meadow.

A cow grazes with her calf. Baby piglets lie near their mother. Their stomachs are full, and they are squealing happily. Noisy ducklings quack. They seem to be saying, "Spring is here!"

As the days of spring pass, the Earth continues its journey around the sun. At this point in the orbit, the position of the Earth's axis makes the Northern Hemisphere tilt toward the sun. Now the North Pole is as close to the sun as it will get. It is the first day of summer.

Because we now receive so much sunlight, the first day of summer is the longest day of the year. This means we have more hours of daylight than at any other time of year. The first day of summer arrives on June 20 or 21.

Spring begins

Summer begins

Winter begins

Sun

Earth's orbit

Autumn begins

The days of summer are long, hot, and lazy. In time, the seeds planted by farmers in spring begin to bear fruit. Cucumbers and carrots and tomatoes are ready to be picked. Summer is a time of ripening.

Flower gardens burst with blooms. Daisies and roses hold up their heads to the golden sunshine.

Ducklings lose their soft, fuzzy down, as their adult feathers fill in. Each day, the babies look more like their mothers and fathers.

The young animals are getting bigger and stronger. They play in the meadow and bask in the sun. While they are playing, they are also learning how to survive. Bear cubs follow their mother. She will teach them to find food to eat, such as berries, and to find shelter. A young fox chases a butterfly. It seems to be playing, but it is also practicing how to hunt.

Butterflies flit and flutter among the flowers. They drink the sweet nectar in the blooms. Orange-and-black monarchs, small white cabbage butterflies, and black swallowtails seem to dance in the summer air.

Honeybees busily gather pollen and nectar from the flowers. Honey must be made, the hive must be tended, and the young bees must be fed.

During summer, most schools are closed. Children are on vacation. It's time to swim, hike, and camp. It's time to dream and to explore.

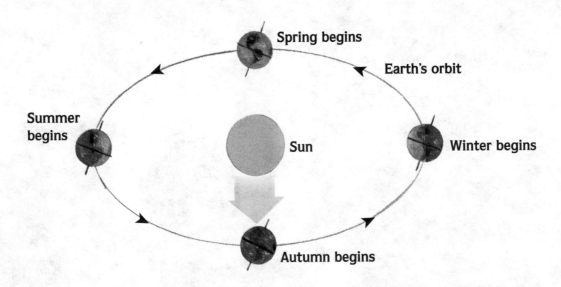

Spring begins

Earth's orbit

Summer begins

Sun

Winter begins

Autumn begins

Gradually, the days grow shorter. The long, dreamy days of summer are drawing to a close. Autumn arrives on September 22 or 23. Once again, the Earth's position has changed because of its trip around the sun.

On the first day of autumn, the sun's rays are right above the equator, as they were in spring. Once again, this causes us to have an equal number of hours of light and darkness. Then, as autumn begins, the North Pole starts to lean away from the sun. In the northern part of the world, days grow shorter.

There is a chill in the air. Flocks of robins settle on the branches of trees. Swallows gather on telephone wires. Everywhere birds cheep and chatter. It is time for the fall migration. During this autumn journey, many birds travel south to where the weather is warm.

Clouds of monarch butterflies join the migration. Some of them will fly all the way from Canada to Mexico.

Chipmunks and squirrels dart here and there. Their cheeks are bulging with nuts and seeds. Squirrels busily bury acorns. On cold winter days, when food is scarce, the squirrels will dig up their hidden treasures to eat.

A lonely caterpillar clings to a branch. It is spinning a cocoon.
Like most of the other caterpillars that are already tucked away, this
caterpillar will spend the long, cold months ahead safe within its
cocoon. Autumn is a time of getting ready for winter.

In autumn, grapes hang heavy on the vine. The trees are thick with golden pears and rosy apples. Pumpkins, fat and orange, lie ripening in the sun.

The fields of corn that are used for grain to feed animals are ready for the harvest. Autumn is a time of reaping. The days pass, and the trees grow bare. The weeds and flowers are withered.

Spring begins

Winter begins

Summer begins

Sun

Autumn begins

Earth's orbit

40

Winter arrives on December 21 or 22. The North Pole is slanting far away from the sun. The first day of winter is the shortest day of the year in the Northern Hemisphere.

Because the sun is lower in the sky, the days are shorter and colder. Snow falls. It fills the empty birds' nests. It covers the trees and houses with a white blanket. When the sun shines, some of the snow melts. Later, when it is colder, the melting snow freezes into glassy icicles.

Not all the birds have flown south. Blue jays, cardinals, and sparrows call to one another. They gather at the feeder and argue over crumbs. Their feet leave little tracks in the snow.

Many frogs have gone to the bottom of the pond to wait for warmer weather.

Chipmunks and bears go to sleep. They will spend the short days and long nights of winter curled up in their cozy winter homes.

Frost and snow have killed many of the insects, but others sleep, or *hibernate*, through the winter. Insect eggs are safe from the winter cold. Some hang in papery nests. Others stay dry in a hollow log or underneath fallen trees.

When spring returns, the insects awaken, the eggs hatch, and the cycle of life continues. Winter is a time of waiting.

The Earth's journey around the sun continues. The seasons come. The seasons go. Winter, spring, summer, autumn—the mysterious and wonderful story of the seasons never ends.

Index

autumn, 5, 9, 46
    signs of, 34–39
    start of, 32
axis, of the Earth, 7 (defined)
    tilt of, 8–9, 22

bears:
    in summer, 27
    and winter hibernation, 44
birds:
    and autumn migration, 34
    babies:
        birth of, 15
        food for, 16
    and spring migration, 13–14
    winter habits of, 42
blue jays, in winter, 42
butterflies:
    monarch, and autumn migration, 35
    in summer, 28

cardinals, in winter, 42
caterpillar, spinning cocoon, 37
children, summer activities of, 30
chipmunks:
    in autumn, 36
    and winter hibernation, 44
cow and calves, in spring, 21
cycle of life, 45

daylight:
    and equal hours of darkness, 11, 32
    longest day, 22
    shortest day, 41

ducklings:
    in spring, 21
    in summer, 26

Earth, moving around the sun, 5–10, 22, 32, 46
    length of journey, 6
equator, 11 (defined), 32

farming:
    in autumn, 38–39
    in spring, 17
    in summer, 24
flowers:
    in autumn, 39
    in spring, 12
    in summer, 25
fox, in summer, 27
frogs, in winter, 43

harvest, in autumn, 38–39
hibernation, 37, 44–45
honeybees, in summer, 29

insects, and winter hibernation, 45

lambs, in spring, 19

migration, 13 (defined), 14, 34–35

North Pole, 7, 8–9, 11, 22, 32, 41
Northern Hemisphere, 8–9, 10, 22, 41, 44–45

orioles, and spring migration, 14

piglets, in spring, 21

rabbits, birth of, in spring, 18
reaping, 39
robins:
    and autumn migration, 34
    and spring migration, 14

scarlet tanagers, and spring migration, 14
seasons:
    cause of, 7–9
    cycle of, 6, 46
    names of, 5
    see also autumn; spring; summer; winter
snow and ice, 41
snow geese, and spring migration, 14
South Pole, 7, 11
sowing, 17
sparrows, in winter, 42
spring, 5, 9, 22, 32, 45, 46
    signs of, 11–21
    start of, 11
squirrels, burying acorns, 36
summer, 5, 9, 32, 46
    signs of, 24–31
    start of, 22
sunlight, 8–9, 22
swallows:
    and autumn migration, 34
    and spring migration, 14

winter, 5, 8, 36, 37, 46
    signs of, 41–45
    start of, 41